The trademark MAGNIFICAT depicted in this publication is used under license from and is the exclusive property of MAGNIFICAT Central Service Team, Inc., A Ministry of Catholic Women, and may not used without its written consent.

**Be Saints!**: Published 2012 by The Incorporated Catholic Truth Society, 40-46 Harleyford Road, London SE11 5AY. www.cts-online.org.uk.

Original text by Pope Benedict XVI copyright © 2010 Libreria Editrice Vaticana. Introductory text and editorial arrangement © 2011 Amy Welborn. Illustrations copyright © 2011 Ann Kissane Engelhart. The Publishers and Illustrator gratefully acknowledge the help of the Waldegrave Drawing Room, St Mary's University College, Strawberry Hill, London, for providing visual references for the illustrations. Layout and design copyright © 2012 The Incorporated Catholic Truth Society. All rights reserved.

Published in 2012 by Ignatius Press, San Francisco • MAGNIFICAT Inc., New York

ISBN Ignatius: 978-1-58617-769-0
ISBN MAGNIFICAT: 978-1-936260-43-0
Printed in Canada ⊗
Printed on 9/2012 by Friesens Corporation, Altona, Manitoba, Canada,
in compliance with the Consumer Protection Safety Act of 2008
Job no. 78413

# Be Saints!

## An Invitation from Pope Benedict XVI

Amy Welborn, *Editor*
Ann Kissane Engelhart, *Illustrator*

MAGNIFICAT.

CTS Children's Books

Ignatius Press

# The Big Assembly

On a bright Friday in September, schoolchildren gathered for an assembly. This happens all the time in school, but this gathering was quite different from the usual: it was the "Big Assembly"—with the Pope!

Yes, the Holy Father, Pope Benedict XVI, had arrived in Great Britain to teach, to pray and to beatify Cardinal John Henry Newman. One of his first stops in England was at St Mary's College in Twickenham. Thousands of children from England, Scotland and Wales had come with their teachers and parents, and even more were watching on television all around the world.

After some beautiful hymns were sung and after some gifts were presented to Pope Benedict, he and the children prayed the Lord's Prayer together. Now it was time for the Holy Father to speak to the children about education, growing in wisdom and what all of their learning and hard work was really all about.

"That they may have life,
and have it abundantly.

*(John 10:10)*

## Future Saints

I hope that among those of you listening to me today there are some of the future saints of the twenty-first century. What God wants most of all for each one of you is that you should become holy. He loves you much more than you could ever begin to imagine, and he wants the very best for you. By far the best thing for you is to grow in holiness.

"Praise to the Holiest in the Height,
And in the depth be praise:
In all his words most wonderful;
Most sure in all his ways."

*Blessed John Henry Newman*

## Pursue One Goal

Perhaps some of you have never thought about this before. Perhaps some of you think being a saint is not for you. Let me explain what I mean. When we are young, we can usually think of people that we look up to, people we admire, people we want to be like. It could be someone we meet in our daily lives that we hold in great esteem. Or it could be someone famous. We live in a celebrity culture, and young people are often encouraged to model themselves on figures from the world of sport or entertainment. My question for you is this: What are the qualities you see in others that you would most like to have yourselves? What kind of person would you really like to be?

"You ask me whether I am in good spirits.
How could I not be so?
As long as faith gives me strength
I will always be joyful."

*Blessed Pier Giorgio Frassati*

## True Happiness

When I invite you to become saints, I am asking you not to be content with second best. I am asking you not to pursue one limited goal and ignore all the others. Having money makes it possible to be generous and to do good in the world, but, on its own, it is not enough to make us happy. Being highly skilled in some activity or profession is good, but it will not satisfy us unless we aim for something greater still. It might make us famous, but it will not make us happy. Happiness is something we all want, but one of the great tragedies in this world is that so many people never find it, because they look for it in the wrong places.

> " What really matters in life is that we are loved
> by Christ, and that we love him in return.
> In comparison to the love of Jesus,
> everything else is secondary. "
>
> *Blessed Pope John Paul II*

## Friendship with God

The key to it is very simple—true happiness is to be found in God. We need to have the courage to place our deepest hopes in God alone, not in money, in a career, in worldly success, or in our relationships with others, but in God. Only he can satisfy the deepest needs of our heart.

"Give me, good Lord, a full faith,
a firm hope, and a fervent charity,
a love to the good Lord incomparable
above the love to myself; and that
I love nothing to thy displeasure,
but everything in an order to thee."

*Saint Thomas More*

13

## The Practice of Virtue

Not only does God love us with a depth and an intensity that we can scarcely begin to comprehend, but he invites us to respond to that love. You all know what it is like when you meet someone interesting and attractive, and you want to be that person's friend. You always hope he will find you interesting and attractive, and want to be your friend. God wants your friendship. And once you enter into friendship with God, everything in your life begins to change.

"Put on then, as God's chosen ones, holy and beloved, heartfelt compassion, kindness, humility, gentleness, and patience, bearing with one another and forgiving one another, if one has a grievance against another; as the Lord has forgiven you, so must you also do. And over all these put on love."

*Saint Paul (Colossians 3:12)*

> "If you have a sick or lonely person at home, be there.
> Maybe just to hold a hand, maybe just to give a smile,
> that is the greatest, the most beautiful work."
>
> *Blessed Mother Teresa*

## Reflect His Infinite Goodness

As you come to know him better, you find you want to reflect something of his infinite goodness in your own life. You are attracted to the practice of virtue. You begin to see greed and selfishness and all the other sins for what they really are, destructive and dangerous tendencies that cause deep suffering and do great damage, and you want to avoid falling into that trap yourselves. You begin to feel compassion for people in difficulties, and you are eager to do something to help them. You want to come to the aid of the poor and the hungry; you want to comfort the sorrowful; you want to be kind and generous. And once these things begin to matter to you, you are well on the way to becoming saints.

## Everything Is Part of the Bigger Picture

In your Catholic schools, there is always a bigger picture over and above the individual subjects you study, the different skills you learn. All the work you do is placed in the context of growing in friendship with God, and all that flows from that friendship... But always remember that every subject you study is part of a bigger picture. Never allow yourselves to become narrow. The world needs good scientists, but a scientific outlook becomes dangerously narrow if it ignores the religious or ethical dimension of life, just as religion becomes narrow if it rejects the legitimate contribution of science to our understanding of the world. We need good historians and philosophers and economists, but if the account they give of human life within their particular field is too narrowly focused, they can lead us seriously astray.

" Be praised, my Lord, through all your creatures,
especially through my lord Brother Sun,
who brings the day; and you give light through him.
And he is beautiful and radiant in all his splendor!
Of you, Most High, he bears the likeness.

Be praised, my Lord, through Sister Moon and the stars;
in the heavens you have made them, precious and beautiful. "

*Saint Francis of Assisi*

## Give Yourself Totally to Jesus

A good school provides a rounded education for the whole person. And a good Catholic school, over and above this, should help all its students to become saints… Dear friends, I thank you for your attention; I promise to pray for you, and I ask you to pray for me.

"I invite you to become Saints!" POPE BENEDICT XVI

SAINT OF THE WEEK

ST. IGNATIUS OF LOYOLA

"Lord, teach me to be generous.
Teach me to serve you as you deserve;
to give and not to count the cost,
to fight and not to heed the wounds,
to toil and not to seek for rest,
to labor and not to ask for reward,
save that of knowing that I do your will."

*Saint Ignatius of Loyola*

Dear young friends:
only Jesus knows what
"definite service" he has in mind for you.
Be open to his voice resounding
in the depths of your heart: even now
his heart is speaking to your heart...

Ask our Lord what he has in mind for you! Ask
him for the generosity to say, "Yes!"
Do not be afraid to give yourself totally to Jesus.
He will give you the grace you need to fulfill
your vocation.

" **We have given up everything and followed you.** "
*Saint Peter (Mark 10:28)*